האָרתו אוב

έλα να δεις

COME AND SEE

A VERSE INTERPRETATION
OF THE GOSPEL OF JOHN

ERIC HOFFMAN

DOS MADRES

2024

DOS MADRES PRESS INC.

P.O. Box 294, Loveland, Ohio 45140
www.dosmadres.com   editor@dosmadres.com

Dos Madres is dedicated to the belief that the small press is essential to the vitality of contemporary literature as a carrier of the new voice, as well as the older, sometimes forgotten voices of the past. And in an ever more virtual world, to the creation of fine books pleasing to the eye and hand.

Dos Madres is named in honor of Vera Murphy and Libbie Hughes, the "Dos Madres" whose contributions have made this press possible.

Dos Madres Press, Inc. is an Ohio Not For Profit Corporation and a 501 (c) (3) qualified public charity. Contributions are tax deductible.

Executive Editor: Robert J. Murphy

Illustration & Book Design: Elizabeth H. Murphy
www.illusionstudios.net

Typeset in Adobe Garamond Pro & Felix Titling
ISBN 978-1-962847-10-0
Library of Congress Control Number: 2024938118

TABLE OF CONTENTS

If we take eternity to mean not infinite temporal duration but timelessness, then eternal life belongs to those who live in the present.

—Ludwig Wittgenstein

Changes in convention can only occur when there are radical changes in the general structure of feeling.

—Raymond Williams

He is risen, renewing the people.

—Commentary from *Ta Hsio*
Ezra Pound, tr.

FOREWORD

The Gospel of John, one of the four Gospels of Jesus Christ, numbers among the most important and influential texts in all of human history. Arguably, it is the Gospel most foundational to Christian theology. The secondary literature that surrounds it is immense, its every word examined in exacting detail, from many angles and within many different contexts.

Though an overall consensus has been reached with regards to both the structure and message of John's Gospel, several controversies remain, mainly with regards to its authorship. For most of its history, these concerns were of considerably less importance to John's audience, which was comprised primarily of the clergy and the lay community. Since at least the third century CE, the author of the Gospel was believed to be John the Apostle, one of the Twelve Apostles of Jesus, the son of Zebedee and brother of James the Apostle, identified within the text—though unnamed—as "the Beloved Disciple." The Gospel was thought to have been composed in the final decades of the first century after the destruction of the Temple of Jerusalem in 70 CE, after which John, in his old age, lived in exile among a community of followers somewhere in Greece; like all the books of the New Testament, John was written in Greek and, furthermore, its content seems intended for a Greek audience. The Gospel of John, the three epistles attributed to John, and the Book of Revelation make up the entirety of what has come to be known as Johannine literature.

In recent decades, scholars grew increasingly skeptical of this authorial tradition, and discussion over the authorship of John's Gospel became contentious. Some modern scholars believe that John of Patmos is the author of Revelations, as opposed to the Apostle, and that only the first of the three epistles attributed to John were written by the same author of the Gospel. Nevertheless, in the early part of the twentieth century, Bishop Westcott, guided by textual evidence in the Johannine literature, made the compelling case that the same author of the Gospel and first epistle also authored Revelations, and that this author was of Jewish and not Greek descent, as previously speculated. Westcott based this conclusion on the author's intimate knowledge of specific geography, literature, and Rabbinic traditions. However, skeptics of apostolic authorship contend that, as the original text was composed in Greek and is not a translation from Hebrew or Aramaic—the languages most familiar to the Apostle John, who was, according to his depiction in the Gospels, an uneducated fisherman—it seems unlikely that John would possess the intellect needed to acquire such a sophisticated understanding of the Greek language and grammar, or indeed the Hellenistic and Platonistic theories of which much of the theology of John is derived. Nevertheless, people of faith maintain that John the fisherman was a much different man than the older and wiser John the Apostle, who was tasked with the deliverance of a divine message, and that his intellectual, theological, and literary talents were themselves gifts from God. Though a consensus cannot currently be reached, most modern scholars agree that the only certainty concerning the author of the Gospel, if it is indeed a single author, is that it is not John the Apostle and neither should the Beloved Disciple mentioned in the text be identified with him.

The Gospel's date of composition, on the other hand, remains generally consistent with the tradition; it has been narrowed down to 70 to 110 CE, or even later. Of the four canonical Gospels, the orthodox view, largely agreed with today, is that John was the last to be composed, preceded by the three Synoptic gospels, Mark, Matthew, and Luke, with which it shares very little commonality, either in form or in content. Where those Gospels are largely concerned with historical representations of Jesus—what he said and did, and his historical personage, i.e. his kingly heritage, religious teachings, and political impact—John's Gospel is an exploration and meditation on what Jesus *represents*, particularly with regards to his followers. This difference is conveyed principally through his Gospel's unique structure, which is much different from the Synoptics. In John, for example, the account of Jesus's brief ministry is lengthened from roughly one calendar year in the Synoptics to three; Jesus is in Jerusalem for Passover on three separate occasions and Jerusalem is the principal location for much of his activities, whereas in the Synoptics he visits Jerusalem only once. There is no Sermon on the Mount in John's Gospel. Instead there are lengthy, decidedly literary dialogues with individuals who appear in no other accounts, and didactic monologues, called the Farewell Discourses, given by Jesus to his disciples. As evidenced by these dialogues and discourses, and by the prologue, with its emphasis on the centrality of the logos—a Greek word meaning "word," "reason," or "plan"—with regards to both God and creation, John's Gospel evinces a decidedly Jewish concern over the importance of the word, specifically God's word in relation to man, which connects this Gospel with examples from the Old Testament, such as the Tower of Babel, the Ten Commandments, the Ark of the Covenant, the Torah and its codification of God's word into law, and the teachings of the Prophets, and with the New Testament, most notably Revelations.

Around the time of the formation of a royal Jewish family with the reign of King David, circa 1000 BCE, the concept of an external God in communication with humanity via the spoken and written word evolved into the messianic idea. This lasted until the destruction of the House of David, c. 586 BCE. Freed from a specific royal personage, the historical messianic concept developed into a dispersed people's abstract hope, wherein an idealized ruler, often a military ruler, will lead the people out from the wilderness and restore the Jewish kingdom. Ezekiel eventually charged this persona with eschatological powers capable of bringing about the end of the world to restore the Kingdom of Heaven on Earth and later, Daniel ascribed this messiah with supernatural powers and the divinity of God. His arrival, Daniel contends, will herald the permeation and synthesis of Earth and Heaven. As above, so below.

John's Gospel is nothing less than an account of Jesus's fulfillment of this promise. The Jesus of John is, from the start, absolutely certain of and without conflict with regards to his divine mission; indeed, the hymn-like prologue to John, which evokes the opening verses of Genesis ("In the beginning was the Word, and the Word was with God, and the Word was God") and therefore, in Judeo-Christian cosmology, the beginning of the universe, likens Christ to the generative *logos*, a wisdom that existed before time and space and whose potential makes all of existence—indeed, even the concept of God itself—possible. As a result, in John, there is no need to establish Jesus's divinity or royal lineage. Note the several occasions Jesus tells his followers "I am"—I am the bread of life; I am the light of the world; I am the door of the sheep; I am the resurrection and the life; I am the good shepherd; I am the way, the truth, and the life; I am the true vine; and Before Abraham was, I am. This Jesus is absolutely certain of his identity and his purpose. There is no account, not even a mention, of Jesus's infancy, so important in the Gospels of Matthew and Luke, to establish Jesus's Davidic lineage. There is no baptism of Jesus by John the Baptist; instead the Baptist need only *bear witness* to Jesus. The cleansing of the temple that in the Synoptics takes place in the final week of Jesus's life, after he enters Jerusalem, in John takes place at the beginning of his ministry. Jesus does not require temptation by Satan in the wilderness, does not require the experience of transfiguration, does not suffer a night of doubt in the Garden of Gethsemane, nor plead with God to be spared his fate on the Cross. After all, the Crucifixion as portrayed in John is not the culmination of the tragic events of the Passion, replete with miraculous events (darkness at noon, an earthquake, the rending of the temple veil, and the resurrection of dead saints), rather it depicts the ecstatic triumph of Christ's divine mission, to which he was fated from the very moment the cosmos began.

The prologue of John announces the permeation of God's divinity in all things with this notion that through the divine word of God all things came into being. The association of Jesus with this word, wherein "the Word was made flesh," is symbolic of the manifestation of the light and wisdom of God's creation within humanity. God and the cosmos he created are no longer remote and external, but are instead suffused within our very being, and share in our humanity. What Jesus in John represents is this mystical unity of God and his creation.

In a text laden with symbolism, Jesus is the ultimate symbol. Indeed, the miracles that Jesus performs are in John referred to semiotically as "signs," that, unlike the Synoptics, are in John ascribed with decidedly metaphorical qualities, which is to say, his miracles are symbolic of the higher consciousness Jesus offers to humanity through a belief in his God-given divinity, in both his words and actions. If God's purpose on Earth is the restoration of Heaven, it is not the result of some eschatological event in the future, as depicted in Ezekiel and Daniel, or indeed by Jesus himself in the "Little Apocalypse" of Mark, but rather of a re-framing of one's spiritual vision, a rending of the veil that separates man from God and God from man. In other words, what Jesus represents above all else to humanity is their capacity to recognize that eternal life already exists within the Earthly Kingdom of Heaven, that the divinity of Christ is as present in the historical moment on Earth as it is in the timeless eternity of Heaven. His Crucifixion, for Christians the central cosmological event, is a reconciliation between God and man, a reaffirmation of the divine that exists within all of us. It is symbolic of the self-sacrifice that ultimately liberates humanity from the existential torment of the nihilism that results when one lives in service of the self as opposed to a higher power, and from the chains of humanly desires, of self-seeking and self-glorification that leads to the ultimate damnation of utter meaninglessness, the darkness within the absence of the light of God's wisdom. It is the freedom from and triumph over the temptations and the bonds of Satan.

John's Gospel, with its emphasis on the word and on symbolic thought, together with the cohesiveness of its structure—its many dialogues and discourses—lends itself to a presentation in verse, specifically the lyric form that predominates English poetry today, and this is initially what inspired my attempt to render John's Gospel in verse. Given the brilliance and economy of the original, the structure was simple enough. John's Gospel is roughly divided into five distinct sections: the aforementioned prelude, Christ's ministry and miracles, called by scholars the *Book of Signs*, Jesus's final discourses to his Apostles and his final prayer, the Passion narrative, and a brief epilogue depicting his resurrection. In some instances, as in the prologue, the verse format is inherent to the original Greek, but most other times, it is most decidedly prose-like, with swathes of descriptive narrative accounts that do not lend themselves easily to the lyric form. This was the primary challenge in this experiment.

Early on, I resolved myself to have each of the twenty-one chapters of John make up individual poems and, for the most part, the original text lends itself to this design. Though there are a few isolated instances where the chapter breaks in the original text needed to be avoided to retain cohesiveness, they are rare and inconsequential enough to not require explication here. Certain sub-sections within chapters naturally presented themselves, as is evident here with the discrete sections that exist within most of the individual poems. Suffice it to say, a number of liberties had to be taken structurally to make the text cohere within the framework as presented.

Of a far more pressing concern than form is the content, most specifically the words themselves. There are dozens of different translations of John's Gospel, of highly varying degrees of quality and literalness. Some are tin–eared, and others, such as the King James, are highly poetic, and contain phrases of such eloquence, beauty, and power that they have become a part of the English lexicon. I did not seek to avoid any specific translation for its lack of merit as any poor translation at least provides examples of various pitfalls in interpretation, literalisms, or errors to avoid. On the other hand, finer, more poetic translations were, somewhat paradoxically, treated with equal caution if only to avoid allowing that translation to overwhelm my own. Occasionally, as in the case of the King James, I retained certain passages or phrases in their entirety as they have attained authority in English and to any alternate translations or interpretations seemed vacant or odd, akin to a revision of a line from Shakespeare. At times, various interpretations from the Greek—with which I am not familiar but with which certain scholarly treatments (principally C.H. Dodd) helped to explicate, often intricately—were equally valid. My solution therefore was to either find a coalescence, if possible, or to simply go with the interpretation(s) that seemed most valid or most adaptable to the lyric form or to the synthesis of the whole. Oftentimes, my choices were based on sonic considerations or matters of personal taste.

This verse interpretation presents John's Gospel in an aesthetically harmonious lyric form. It is an experiment, not an exercise in scholarship. As a result, there are no scholarly restrictions that take precedence over the lyric. The results of this experiment stand here before you, not as witness or as guide, rather as accompaniment. The words of John are keys meant to be played by the soul. They are essential ingredients for the development and refinement of the Everlasting Spirit. Perhaps in some defiance to poetic values, these lyrics stand as unadorned as possible, so that each acuminated image and phrase intends, as did the original Greek, to pierce the thin veil between the human and the divine, and to allow the Gospel's symbols and metaphors, so essential to poetic discourse, to stand before us transparent as glass. Come and see.

Further Reading

Brown, Raymond E. *The Gospel According to John*. 2 volumes. New Haven, CT: Yale University Press, 1970.
Dodd, C.H. *Historical Tradition in the Fourth Gospel*. Cambridge: Cambridge University Press, 1963.
—*The Interpretation of the Fourth Gospel*. Cambridge: Cambridge University Press, 1954.
Westcott, B.F. *The Gospel According to St. John*. London: John Murray, 1908.

האָרטו אוב

έλα να δεις

COME AND SEE

NARTHEX

Let this mind be in you, which was also in Christ Jesus:

Who, being in the form of God, thought it not robbery to be equal with God:

made himself of no reputation, and took upon him the form of a servant, and was made in the likeness of men:

And being found in fashion as a man, he humbled himself, and became obedient unto death, even the death of the Cross.

Wherefore God also hath highly exalted him, and given him a name which is above every name:

That at the name of Jesus every knee should bow, of things in Heaven, and things in earth, and things under the earth;

And that every tongue should confess that Jesus Christ is Lord, to the glory of God the Father.

Philippians 2:5–11

PROLOGUE

In the beginning was λόγος
The thought and the Word

And the Word was God
And the Word was with God in the beginning

And the Word brought all things into being
Nothing exists that the Word does not make

And the Word was life
And life was the Light of mankind

The Light shines in the darkness
And the darkness cannot extinguish the Light

NAVE

ONE

1.

There arose, became
A man from God named John

To witness the Light
So that all might believe.

He was not the Light
But came for testimony,

The true Light that shines
On all was born into this world.

He did not bring the Word
Already come into the world,

Unrecognized and unwelcomed
By His own people.

Those that did receive Him,
Born not of flesh, nor of blood,

Nor the will of man,
Became the children of God.

And the Word became flesh.
And He fixed His tent among us.

And we witnessed the Glory
Shared by Father and Son.

And the Word was filled
With grace and truth.

2.

Behold, said John,
The one who follows

Is of greater rank than I
Because He preceded me,

And from His abundance
We have received,

And grace for grace.
For Moses gave the law,

But grace and truth
Come from Jesus Christ.

No one has seen God.
The only begotten Son,

Close to His father's side,
Has revealed Him.

3.

This is the testimony of John
When the Pharisees from Jerusalem
Sent priests and Levites to question him,
To ask of him who he was:

I am not the Messiah, the Christ,
The anointed one, he said plainly.
Are you Elijah? No.
Are you the prophet? No.

We need a reply to bring back
To those that sent us. Who are you?
I am the voice of one crying in the wilderness,
Make straight the way of the Lord.

Some Pharisees had also been sent
To question him. And they asked him,
If you are not the Christ, how do you baptize?
I baptize with water, he replied.

One stands among you, whom you do not recognize.
He is the one who comes after me,
Whose sandal strap I am not fit to untie.
This happened in Bethany, across the Jordan.

The next day, John saw Jesus approach.
Behold! He cried. The Lamb of God
Who takes away the sin of the world!
This is He of whom I spoke when I said

The one who follows me is of greater rank
Because He preceded me.
I did not know Him, but came to Israel
To baptize with water so that He may be revealed.

And as John bare record, I saw the spirit
Descend from Heaven like a dove,
And rest upon Him. I did not know Him.
But the one who sent me to baptize with water

Said unto me, on whomever you see
The spirit descend and rest upon Him,
He will baptize with the Holy Spirit.
I have seen and testify that this is the Son of God.

4.

The next day, John was standing there again
With two of his disciples
When he saw Jesus walking by and cried,

Behold, the Lamb of God!
When John's disciples heard this,
They followed Jesus. He turned

And saw them following Him.
What do you seek? He demanded.
They said to him, Rabbi, where do You dwell?

He said, Come and see.
So they went, and saw,
And remained with Him, as it was late.

One was Andrew, the brother of Simon Peter.
He found his brother Simon and said,
We have found the Messiah, the Christ.

Andrew brought Simon to Jesus,
Who looked upon him and said,
You will be called Cephas (Peter, a stone).

The next day, Jesus went to Galilee,
And there found Philip, who,
Like Andrew and Peter, was from Bethesda.

Follow Me, Jesus said.
Philip found Nathanael and said,
We have found the one Moses wrote about

In the Torah, and the prophets:
Jesus, the son of Joseph of Nazareth.
Can anything good come out of Nazareth?

Nathanael asked. Philip said,
Come and see.
When Jesus saw Nathanael approach,

He said, Here is an Israelite without deceit.
How do you know me? Nathanael asked.
Before Philip brought you, He replied,

I saw you beneath the fig tree.
Nathanael said, Rabbi, You are the Son of God,
The King of Israel.

You believe because I saw you
Beneath the fig tree, Jesus said.
But you will see greater things than these.

You will see the heavens open,
And the angels of God ascending
And descending upon the Son of Man.

TWO

1.

And on the third day there was a wedding
In Cana in Galilee.
And Mary mother of Jesus was there.
Jesus and His Disciples were also invited.

And when the wine ran out, Mary told Jesus.
And Jesus said to Mary, Woman,
Of what concern is this to us?
My hour is not yet come.

So Mary told the servants,
Do whatever my Son tells you.
Six stone waterpots, there for purification,
Held two or three firkins each.

Jesus commanded the servants
To fill each of them to the brim. And so they did.
Then He said, pour some out
And bring it to the master of the feast.

And so they did. The master tasted it,
And it tasted like wine, for it was wine.
He did not know from where it came,
Though the servants did.

He called to the bridegroom
And said to him, it is customary
To serve the good wine first,
But you have waited till the last.

This was the first of Jesus's miraculous signs
In Cana in Galilee.
He made manifest His glory and in witness
Of this His disciples believed in Him.

2.

After this, He went down to Capernaum,
Together with His Mother and His many disciples,
And they stayed there not many days.

Jewish Passover approached,
And Jesus went up to Jerusalem.
In the temple, He discovered people

Who sold oxen, sheep, and doves,
And the money changers seated there.
From small cords, Jesus fashioned a scourge

And with it drove them from the temple
And overturned the money changers' tables,
Scattering their coins. He exhorted

To those who sold the doves,
Take these things away!
Do not make My father's house a marketplace!

His disciples remembered that it is written,
Zeal for your house consumes me.
The Jewish leaders asked Him,

What sign can You provide
That gives You authority to do such things?
Jesus answered, Destroy this temple

And in three days' time I will raise it up.
The Jews said, It took forty-six years
To build this temple, and You will raise it in three?

But Jesus spoke of the temple of His body.
After His resurrection from the dead,
His disciples remembered these words

And they believed the scripture
And the words that Jesus spoke.
When He was in Jerusalem

At the time of the Passover feast,
Many people saw His signs
And came to believe in Him.

But Jesus did not entrust Himself to them
Because He knew human nature.
He required no testimony: He understood.

THREE

1.

There was a Pharisee named Nicodemus,
One of the Sanhedrin, a ruler of the Jews,
Who came to Jesus at night and said,
Rabbi, we know You are a teacher come from God,
For no one without God could perform these miracles.
Jesus answered, Amen, amen, I say to you:
Unless a man be born anōthen,
He cannot see the Kingdom of God.

Nicodemus said, How can one be born again
When he is old? He cannot return
To his mother's womb to be born a second time.
Jesus answered, Amen, amen,
Unless he is born of water and the Spirit,
He cannot enter the Kingdom of God.
That which is born of flesh is flesh,
That which is born of the Spirit is spirit.

Do not marvel that I have said to you,
You must be born again.
The wind bloweth where it listeth,
Yet you cannot hear its sound
Or determine its origin or fate.
The same may be said of those born of the Spirit.
Nicodemus said, How can these things be?
Jesus said, you are a great teacher of Israel

Yet you do not understand these things?
Amen, amen, I say to you: we speak
Of what we know and testify what we see,
Yet you refuse to accept our testimony.
If I speak of earthly things and you do not believe,
How will you believe if I speak of heavenly things?
No one has ascended to Heaven,
But one has come down: the Son of Man.

And as Moses in the wilderness
Lifted up the brass serpent,
So the Son of Man must be lifted up,
So that whomever believes in Him
Will not perish but will have eternal life.
For God so loves the world that He gave his only Son,
So that whomever believes in Him
Will not perish but have everlasting life.

For God did not send His Son into the world
To condemn the world but that through Him the world might be saved.
He who believes is not condemned,
Yet he that does not believe is already condemned
because he does not believe
in the name of the only Son.
And this is the judgment, that the light
Has come into the world, yet men

Loved darkness instead of light,
Because their deeds were evil.
For those who do evil hate the light
And refuse to come into the light
Lest their evil be exposed.
But those who practice truth come out into the Light,
That their deeds may be made manifest,
That they are wrought in God.

2.

After this, Jesus and His disciples
Came into the Judean wilderness,

And there He remained to baptize.
And John was baptizing in Aenon near Salim,

Where there was much water.
And the people came to him to be baptized.

John was not yet imprisoned.
There arose an argument between a Jew

And John's disciples over the ritual
Of purification, of ceremonial washing.

And the disciples went to John and said,
Rabbi, the Man who was with you

On the other side of the Jordan,
The Man about whom you testified,

He baptizes, and the people now go to Him.
John responded, A man receives nothing

Unless it is given to him from Heaven.
You yourselves bore witness when I said

I am not the Messiah; I am only the one
Sent before Him. The bridegroom

Has the bride, but the bridegroom's friend
Rejoices at the sound of his voice.

My pleasure and my joy are now complete.
His importance increases as mine withdraws.

He that comes from Heaven is utmost,
While he that is of the earth can speak

Only of the earth. He that comes from Heaven
Is consummate. And He testifies

To what He has seen and heard,
Yet no one receives His Testimony.

Those that do set their seal to *this*,
That God is truth. For the one God sent

Speaks God's words, because God gives
The Spirit generously. The Father loves His Son

And has entrusted Him with the world.
He that believes in Him has life everlasting,

And he that does not does not see,
And the wrath of God abides within him.

FOUR

1.

The Lord learned that the Pharisees had heard
That He had baptized more disciples than John,
Though Jesus did not baptize; His disciples did.
He departed Judea and left for Galilee,

Passing through Samaria. He came to Shechem,
Close to that place that Jacob gave Joseph.
Jacob's Well was there, and Jesus, travel-wearied,
Sat down by the well to rest. It was almost noon.

A Samaritan woman came to the well to draw water.
Jesus said to her, Give me water to drink.
His disciples had gone into the city for meat.
She replied to Him, How is that You, Jew,

Ask me, a Samaritan woman, for a drink?
Jesus answered, If only you knew the gift of God
And who it is that asks you for a drink,
You would ask Him instead,

And He would have given you living water.
She said, You have nothing with which to draw,
And the well is deep. Are you a greater father
Than Jacob, who gave us this well

From which he drank, and fed his sons and cattle?
Jesus said, All who drink of this water
Will forever thirst, but those who drink
The water I provide will never thirst,

And My water will spring eternal life.
She said to Him, Sir, give me this water,
That I shall never thirst, nor need to return
To this well to draw water.

Jesus said, Go, call your husband, and return.
I have no husband, she replied.
Jesus said, You speak truthfully,
For you have had five husbands,

And the man with which you live is not one.
You are a prophet, she said. Our fathers
Worshiped on this mountain, and you Jews say
Jerusalem is where all men ought to worship.

Jesus said, Woman, believe me, when the hour comes
You will worship the Father neither in Jerusalem
Nor on this mountain. You Samaritans worship
What you do not know. We Jews worship

What we know, because salvation comes
From the Jews. Yet a time will come, now,
When true worshippers will worship
The Father in spirit and in truth.

For the Father wants such worshippers.
God is a Spirit, and those who worship Him
Must worship Him in both spirit and truth.
The woman said, I know that a Messiah comes

Who will reveal to us all we need to know.
Jesus said, You speak of Me.
His disciples returned and were astonished to find
Jesus in conversation with this Samaritan woman.

Yet none asked why He spoke with her.
Then the woman left her water-jar,
And returned to the town. She said to the men,
Come and see a Man who told me all things

I ever did. Can this be the Christ, the Messiah?
The men left the city and came to Him.
Meanwhile, His disciples begged Him to eat.
But He said, I have meat that you have not seen.

The disciples asked one another, did you feed Him?
Jesus said, My meat is the will of Him who sent Me,
To accomplish the work He gave Me.
Do not say, There are still four months until harvest.

Behold, I tell you, Lift up your eyes,
And look upon the fields and *see*,
For they are white and ready for harvest.
Already the reaper receives his pay

And gathers fruit for eternal life,
So that those who reap and sow
Can rejoice as one. For the saying is true:
One sows while another reaps.

I sent you to harvest a crop that you have not toiled.
Many Samaritans came to believe in Him
Because of the woman who said,
He told me all I ever did.

So when the Samaritans came to Him,
They asked if they could remain with Him,
And so He remained there for two days.
And many more believed because of His word,

And they said to the woman, Now we believe,
For we have heard Him speak ourselves,
And we know that He is indeed the Christ,
The Savior of the world.

2.

And on the third day, He left Samaria
And went to Galilee. For He testified,
A prophet has no honor in his own country.

So when He arrived in Galilee, they received Him,
For they had seen what He had done
In Jerusalem at the feast.

So Jesus returned to Cana in Galilee
Where He had turned water into wine.
And there in Capernaum was a certain royal

Whose son was mortally ill. When he learned
That Jesus has come from Judea to Galilee,
He went to meet with Him and to plead

That Jesus come down and heal his son.
Unless you see signs and wonders, Jesus said,
You will not believe. The nobleman said,

Come down before my child dies.
Jesus said, Go home. Your son lives.
The official believed Him and departed.

As he approached his home, he was met
By his servants who declared, Your son lives.
So the nobleman asked at what hour his son

Began to heal. Yesterday at one o'clock
In the afternoon, they said. So the father knew
That was the same hour in which Jesus told him,

Your son lives. He believed, as did his house.
This is the second miracle Jesus performed
When He had come out of Judea into Galilee.

FIVE

Later, there was a Jewish feast, and Jesus went to Jerusalem.
By the Sheep Gate there is a pool called Bethesda,
Which has five colonnades. In these lay
A great multitude of people, sick, blind, lame, withered,
Who await the water's movement.

[For at certain seasons an angel of the Lord
Goes down and troubles the water.
The first who enters the troubled water is healed.]
And a certain man lay there beside the pool,
Infirm for thirty-eight long years.

Jesus saw him, and knew that he had been ill
For all that time. He said to him,
Do you want to be healed? The man said,
There is no one to place me in the water
When it is stirred. When I try to enter,

Another enters before me. Jesus said,
Arise, take up thy bed and walk.
And the man was healed, and he gathered his bed
And walked. That day was the Sabbath.
The Jews said to the healed man, it is the Sabbath,

It is unlawful for you to carry your bed.
He answered, The Man who healed me
Instructed me to take up my bed and walk.
They asked him, Who was this man?
The healed man did not know, for Jesus

Had slipped away back into the crowd.
Later, Jesus found him in the temple and said,
Behold, you are healed. Sin no more,
Lest a worse fate occur. The man departed,
And he told the Jews that it was Jesus who healed him.

And for this reason the Jews sought to persecute Jesus,
Because He had healed on the Sabbath.
Yet Jesus answered, My Father works, and I work.
And for this the Jews sought to kill him,
For he said the God was His Father,

And made himself equal with God, a blasphemy.
Jesus answered them, I say to you in truth,
The Son cannot act of His own accord.
He does only what He sees the Father doing,
For what the Father does, the Son does also.

For the Father loves the Son and shows Him
All that He does, and will show Him
Greater works than these, and you will marvel.
For as the Father raises up the dead
And grants them life, so the Son gives life

To whom He will. For the Father judges none,
But has entrusted judgment to His Son,
That all men shall honor the Son as they honor
The Father. Whomever fails to honor the Son
Fails to honor the Father who sent Him.

I speak in truth, he that hears My Word
And believes in Him that sent me,
Shall have eternal life without judgment
And will be resurrected. The hour comes
When the dead shall hear the voice of the Son of God,

And those who hear it shall live.
For as the Father has life in Himself,
So the Son shall also, and He has given him
The authority to judge, for He is the Son of Man.
Do not marvel at this, for the hour comes

In which the entombed shall hear His voice
And shall rise—they that have done good
To a resurrection of life, but those who did evil
To a resurrection of judgment. I myself
Can do nothing. As I hear, I judge,

And My judgment is righteous,
Because I do not seek My own will,
But the will of Him who sent Me.
If I testify of Myself, My testimony is not true.
Another testifies of Me, and his witness is true.

You have inquired of John, and he has testified
The truth. But the testimony that I receive
Does not come from man.
I say these things that you might be saved.
John was a lamp that burned and shined,

And for a while you rejoiced in his light.
But I have a greater witness than John,
For the works that the Father has appointed Me
To accomplish are proof that He has sent Me.
And the Father that sent Me, bears witness of Me.

You have never seen Him or heard His voice.
You do not have His Word within you
Because you do not believe in the one He sent.
Search the Scriptures, because you think
They give you eternal life, and yet

They testify of Me, and you will not come to Me,
That you might have life. I do not receive
Glory from men. But I know you,
That you have no love for God within you.
I come in my Father's name, and you do not

Receive Me. If another comes in My name,
You will accept him. How can you believe,
Who receive glory from another, and not seek
The glory that comes from the only God?
Do not think that I will accuse you before Him.

Moses, in whom you have placed your hope,
Already accuses you. For if you believe Moses,
You would believe Me, for he wrote of Me.
Yet if you do not believe and trust his words,
How will you believe Mine?

SIX

1.

Months later, Jesus crossed the Sea of Galilee.
A great multitude followed Him there,
For they had seen the signs He performed
By healing the sick. Then Jesus climbed a mountain,
And there He sat down with His disciples.

The Jewish feast of the Passover drew near.
Jesus looked up and saw the crowd approach.
He said to Philip, where might we buy bread
Enough that we can feed these many people?
Yet He only said this to test him,

For He already knew what it is that He would do.
Philip responded, Two hundred denarii's worth
Would not provide enough for even a single bite.
Andrew, Simon Peter's brother, said to Jesus,
A boy here has five barley loaves and two fish.

But what are they to so many? Jesus said,
Tell the people to sit. Jesus took the loaves,
Gave thanks (eucharisteō), broke the bread
And gave them to His disciples to distribute.
And also the fish, as much as they wanted.

And when they had eaten enough,
Jesus instructed His disciples to gather
The fragments that remained, that nothing be lost.
So they gathered them and filled twelve baskets
With pieces leftover by those who had eaten

From the five loaves. And when the people
Witnessed this sign, they cried, it must be truth
That this *is* the prophet come into the world.
When Jesus saw that they meant to seize Him
And make Him king, He escaped to the mountains, alone.

2.

That evening, His disciples went down to the sea,
Boarded a boat and set sail for Capernaum.

It was dark, and Jesus had not yet returned.
The wind blew strong and stirred the sea.

After they had rowed nearly thirty stadia,
They saw Jesus walk upon the water.

He came near the boat and made them afraid.
He said to them, Do not be afraid. It is I.

Willingly, they took him on board, and all at once
They arrived upon the shore at their destination.

3.

The next day, the crowd that remained
On the other side of the sea realized
That there was only one boat and that Jesus
Did not board it with His disciples, that they
Had gone away alone. Other boats arrived

From Tiberias near the place they had eaten
The bread after the Lord gave thanks.
And when the crowd saw that Jesus
And His disciples were no longer there,
They boarded boats and sailed to Capernaum,

Seeking Jesus. When they found Him
On the other side of the sea, they said to Him,
Rabbi, when did you come here? Jesus said,
Truly, I say to you, you seek Me, not because
You witnessed the signs, but because you ate

The loaves and were filled. Do not labor
For the meat that perishes. Do not labor for the food
Which perishes, labor for the food
That endures for an eternal life.
The Son of Man will provide this to you,

Because God the Father has set His seal on Him
And marked Him with approval.
They said to Him, What should we do
To also perform God's work?
Jesus answered, the work of God

Is to believe in the One whom He has sent.
They said, Perform a miracle, so that we may believe.
Our fathers ate manna in the desert, and
He gave them bread from Heaven to eat.
Jesus said, Moses did not give you bread

From Heaven. My father did. And now
He brings you the true bread from Heaven.
For the true bread is that which comes down
From Heaven and brings life to the world.
They said, Lord, give us this bread.

Jesus told them, I am the bread of life.
Whoever believes in Me will never hunger or thirst.
Yet, as I have said to you, you have seen Me
And still you are filled with disbelief.
All those My Father gives me will come to Me

And I will never cast them out. For I have come
From Heaven not to do My will but the will
Of the One who sent Me. And it is His will
That I will not lose any of whom He has given,
And that I shall resurrect them on the last day.

And this is the will of Him that sent Me,
That everyone who sees the Son, and believes
Will have everlasting life, and I will raise them up
On the last day. Now the Jews murmured
And found fault with Him because He said,

I am the bread that came down out of Heaven.
And they said, Is this not Jesus, the Son of Joseph,
Whose mother and father we know?
How can He say, I came down from Heaven?
Jesus said, Stop all that murmuring.

No one may come to Me unless the Father sent them,
And I will raise them up on the last day.
It is written in the prophets, *And they shall all be taught by God.*
Therefore, everyone who has heard and learned
From the Father comes to Me. No one

Has seen the Father except He who is from God.
I speak truthfully to you: those who believe in Me
Will have eternal life. I am the bread of life.
Your fathers ate manna in the wilderness and died.
Those who eat the bread from Heaven will not die.

I am the living bread come down from Heaven.
If anyone eats this bread, they will live forever.
The bread is My flesh, which I will give
For the life of the world. The Jews said,
How can this Man give us His flesh to eat?

Jesus said to them, Verily, verily, I say to you,
Unless you eat the flesh of the Son of Man
And drink His blood, you have no life in you.
Whoever eats My flesh and drinks My blood
Has eternal life, and I will raise them up on the last day.

For My flesh is bread, and My blood is wine.
Whomever eats My flesh and drinks My blood
Abides in Me, and I in him. As the living Father sent Me,
And I live because of the Father,
So whoever eats My flesh, will live because of Me.

I am the true bread that came down from Heaven.
Anyone who eats this bread will not die
As your fathers did but will live forever.
Jesus said these things in the synagogue at Capernaum.
His disciples said, Who can accept this difficult teaching?

Jesus said to them, Does it offend you?
What then if you see the Son of Man ascend
To where He was before? The Spirit gives life
Yet the flesh accomplishes nothing.
The words I have spoken to you are spirit and life,

Yet some of you refuse to believe.
This is why I have told you that no one can come to Me
Unless it has been granted him by the Father.
Because He said this, many disciples abandoned Him.
Then Jesus asked the Twelve, Will you leave too?

Simon Peter answered, Where will we go?
You have the words of eternal life.
We believe that you are the Holy One of God.
Jesus said, Did I not choose you?
And yet one of you is a devil.

SEVEN

1.

After this, Jesus traveled throughout Galilee.
He did not want to walk in Judea, for the Jews
Sought to have Him killed.

Yet the Feast of Tabernacles neared,
And His brothers said to Him, Leave Galilee and go to Judea
So that your disciples there might be witness

To your works, for no one who wishes to be seen
Does anything in secret. For not even His brothers
Believed in Him. Jesus replied, My time

Has not yet come, but yours is already at hand.
The world cannot hate you as it hates Me,
Because I testify that its servants are evil.

Go up to the Feast. I will not go up, for My time
Has not arrived. Jesus remained in Galilee.
Yet when His brothers had gone up to the Feast,

He too went, though in secret. The Jews
Searched for Him there, and said, Where is He?
The crowd murmured about Him. Some said

He is a good man, while others disagreed,
And said that He led the people astray.
Yet none spoke openly of Him, for fear of the Jews.

2.

In the midst of the feast, Jesus went to the temple
And taught. The Jews marveled at this, and said,
How is it that this Man is so learned,
Having never studied the Torah?
Jesus answered them, My teaching is not My own,

But of the One who sent me. Anyone who desires
To do the will of God will know if My teaching
Is from God or my own authority. The one
Who speaks from himself seeks his own glory,
But the one who speaks from God seeks the glory of God.

He is true. There is no unrighteousness or falsity
Within Him. Did not Moses bring you the law,
Yet none of you keep it? Why *do* you seek to kill Me?
The crowd answered Him, You have a demon!
Who seeks to kill You? Jesus said,

I have performed one miracle on the Sabbath,
And you are all astonished. Yet you too work
On the Sabbath, when you circumcise a man
According to the gift of Moses
(Not that it is from Moses, but from the Patriarchs,

For their Law existed long before Moses' Law.)
If a man can be circumcised on the Sabbath
And the Law of Moses not broken,
Why are you angry with Me for restoring a man
On the Sabbath? Do not judge Me arrogantly

Or based on superficial appearances.
Judge with righteous judgment, justfully
And with truth. Some of the people
Of Jerusalem said, Is this whom they seek to kill?
Yet here He speaks openly, and no one argues.

Do the Elders know that He is the Messiah?
But we know where He is from. When Christ arrives,
No one will know from where He came.
Jesus cried out, You know Me, and you know
From where I came. I have not come of Myself,

But the One having sent Me is true,
Whom you do not know. I know Him,
For I am from Him, and He has sent Me.
At this, the authorities tried to seize Him,
Yet no one laid a hand on Him.

His hour had not yet come.
Many in the crowd believed Him. They asked,
When the Christ comes, will He perform
More miracles than this Man?
The Pharisees overheard these whisperings

And sent the Temple guards to arrest Him.
Jesus said, I will only be with you a little while longer,
And then I will return to the One who sent Me.
You will search for Me, yet I will not be found.
And where I am, you cannot come.

The Jewish leaders spoke amongst themselves,
Where will He be that we cannot find Him?
Will He go to Diasporic Greece, and teach
The Greeks? What does He mean when He says,
You will search for me, yet I will not be found,
And where I am, you cannot come?

3.

On the last day of the Feast, the greatest day,
Jesus stood and cried, If anyone thirst, let him
Come to Me and let him drink who believes in Me.
As the Scripture says, *From His belly will flow*

Rivers of living water. Jesus spoke of the Spirit,
Whom those that believe in Him should receive;
For the Holy Ghost was not yet given,
Because Jesus was not yet glorified.

Some of the multitude heard these words
And said, Truly this is the Prophet. Others said,
This is the Christ. Yet others asked, Is the Christ
To come from Galilee? Does the Scripture not say

That the Christ is to be descended from David,
And from Bethlehem, where David was?
There was division in the crowd because of Him.
Some wanted to seize Him, yet no one laid hands on Him.

The officers returned to the chief priests
And Pharisees. The priests asked the officers,
Why did you not return with Him? They answered,
No one ever spoke like this Man.

The Pharisees said, Are you also deceived?
Have any of the Pharisee rulers believed in Him?
This crowd does not know the law. They are cursed.
Nicodemus, the ruler who met Jesus earlier, said,

Does our law judge a man before it hears his testimony?
And before it knows what he does? They replied,
Are you from Galilee, too? Read the Scripture
And see that no prophet comes from Galilee.

EIGHT

1.

The meeting then ended, and all went home,
while Jesus went to the Mount of Olives.

Early the next morning, He arrived again
Near the temple. The people returned to Him,

And He sat down to teach them.
The scribes and Pharisees brought Him

A woman who stood accused of adultery
And they made her stand in the middle of the crowd.

They said to Him, Teacher, this woman
Was caught in the act of adultery.

According to Moses' Law, such women
Are to be stoned. What do you say?

This was meant to test Jesus, so that
They might level a charge against Him.

Jesus crouched down and with His finger
Began to write on the ground. When they

Continued to question Him, He stood and said,
Let ye without sin cast the first stone.

Then He bent down and resumed to write.
In response, the scribes and Pharisees

Began to leave, beginning with the elders.
Jesus was left alone with the woman.

He stood again and asked, Woman,
Where did they go? Did no one judge you?

She replied, No. Jesus said, Neither do I
Condemn you. Go, and sin no more.

2.

Then Jesus spoke to the scribes and Pharisees,
Saying, I am the light of the world.
He who follows Me will not dwell in darkness,

But will have the light of life.
The Pharisees said to Him,
You testify of Yourself, yet your testimony is not true.

Jesus said, though I testify of Myself, My testimony is true.
I know where I am from and where I must go.
You do not know where I am from or where I will go.

Your judgments are of the flesh. I judge no one.
Yet even if I was to judge, My judgment is true
Because I am not alone. I am with the Father

That sent me. It is written in your law
That the testimony of two is true. I am One
Who bears witness of myself, and the Father

Who sent Me testifies of Me.
The Pharisees said to Him, Where is this Father?
Jesus said, Since you do not know who I am,

You cannot know who My Father is.
If you knew Me, you would also know My Father.
Jesus spoke these words while He taught

In the Temple, near the treasury, and none
Attempted to seize Him, for His time had not yet come.
Then He said, I will leave you, and you will seek

To find Me, and will die in sin.
Where I go you cannot come. The Jews said,
Will He kill himself? Because He says,

Where I will go you cannot come.
Jesus said, You are from below, I am from above.
You are of this world, I am not.

This is why I said you will die in your sins.
Unless you believe that I am He, you will die in your sins.
The Jews said to Him, Who are you?

Jesus said, Even the same that I said to you
In the beginning. I have much to say of you,
And much to judge, but the One who sent me

Is true, and what I have heard from Him
I will speak to the world. They did not understand
That He spoke of the Father. Then Jesus said,

When you lift up the Son of Man on the Cross,
You will understand that I am He. I do nothing
On My own authority. I do nothing on My own

And only speak what My Father taught Me.
He that sent Me is always with Me.
He has not left Me, because I always do

What He pleases Him. As He spoke these words,
Many came to believe Him.
To the Jews who believed Him, Jesus said,

If you continue in My words, then you are My disciples,
And you shall know the truth,
And the truth shall set you free.

They answered Him, we are the descendants of Abraham
And have never been the slaves of anyone.
How can You say, You will be set free?

Jesus said, I speak the truth when I say to you,
All who sin are the slaves of sin.
A slave does not live in a house forever, yet a Son does.

So if the Son sets you free, you will be free indeed.
I know that you are the sons of Abraham,
Yet you seek ways to kill Me because My word

Has no place within you.
I tell you what I have seen with My Father,
And you do what you have seen with your father.

Abraham is our father, the Jews answered.
Jesus said, If Abraham is your father,
then you would do the deeds of Abraham.

But now you seek to kill Me, a Man who speaks
The truth heard from God. This Abraham did not do.
You do the deeds of your father. They said to Him,

We are not born of fornication. We have but one Father,
God. Jesus said, If God were your father,
You would love Me, as I have come from God.

I did not come of My own accord, for He has sent me.
Why is it that you do not understand My word?
It is because you cannot bear to hear My message.

Your father is the devil, and you act as he desires.
He was a murderer in the beginning, and because
He is full of lies; he cannot stand in truth.

When he lies, he speaks to his own nature,
Because he is a liar, and the father of liars.
I speak the truth, and you do not believe Me.

Who among you can convict Me of sin?
If I speak truth, why is it you do not believe Me?
One from God hears God's words.

You do not listen, because you are not from God.
The Jews answered, Are we not correct when we say
You are a Samaritan possessed by demons?

Jesus answered, I am not possessed.
I honor My Father, and you dishonor Me.
I do not seek glory for Myself.

There is one who seeks glory for Me and judges those
Who dishonor Me. Truly I say to you,
If a man keeps My word, he will never taste death.

The Jews said, Now we know that You are possessed
By a demon. Abraham died, as did the prophets,
Yet You say, If My word is kept, you will not taste death.

Are You greater than Abraham and the prophets, who died?
Jesus answered, If I honor Myself, My honor
Is nothing. It is My Father that honors Me;

Of whom you say, that he is your God.
Though you do not know Him, I know Him.
If I said I did not, I would be a liar like you,

But I do know Him and obey His word.
Your father Abraham rejoiced to see My day
And he saw it, and was glad.

The Jews said, You are not yet fifty years old,
And have You seen Abraham? Jesus said,
Truly, I say to you, before Abraham was, I AM (Yeshua).

The Jews took up stones to cast at Him,
Yet Jesus hid Himself, and went out of the temple,
Through the midst of them, and so passed by.

NINE

And as Jesus passed by, He saw a man
Blind from birth. Jesus' disciples asked,

Rabbi, is this man blind because of the sins
Of his mother and father? Or his own?

Jesus said, Neither. This man is blind
So that God's work might be revealed in him.

We must perform God's work in daylight,
For when night comes, no man can work.

As long as I am in this world, I am its light.
Then He spit on the ground, made clay,

And spread it over the blind man's eyes.
Jesus told him, Go wash in the pool of Siloam.

Neighbors who had seen him blind then asked,
Is this the same man who sat here and begged?

Some said he was, while others disagreed
And said, He just looks like him. And yet

The blind man protested and said, I am he.
So they said to him, How were your eyes opened?

He answered, The man named Jesus made clay
And anointed my eyes, then told me to go

To Siloam and wash. So I did, and received sight.
They asked, Where is He? I do not know, he said.

They brought the blind man to the Pharisees.
Jesus made the clay and opened his eyes

On the Sabbath. The Pharisees asked the man
How he regained his sight. He placed clay on my eyes,

He replied, and I washed, and now I see.
Some of the Pharisees said, This Man

Is not from God. He does not keep the Sabbath.
Others said, How can a man filled with sin

Perform these signs? They were divided.
They asked the blind man, What do you say

Of Him? He opened your eyes. He replied,
He is a prophet. The Jews did not believe

That he was blind and received sight,
Until his parents were summoned.

They asked, Is this your son, whom you say
Was born blind? How does he now see?

He is our son, they said, and he was born blind.
How he now sees, or who opened his eyes,

We do not know. Ask him. He is old enough
To speak on his own behalf. The parents

Said this because they feared the Jews,
As they already concluded that anyone

Confessed Him to be the Christ,
They would be cast out of the synagogue.

A second time, the Jews called the blind man,
And said, Give glory to God. We know this Man

Is a sinner. The blind man said, I do not know
If He is a sinner, only that I was blind and now

I see. They inquired, What did He do to you?
How did He open your eyes? The man replied,

I already told you, yet you did not hear me.
Why must I tell you again? Do you want

To become His disciples? They ridiculed him,
Heaped insults upon him, and said,

You are His disciple. We are the disciples
Of Moses. We know that God spoke to Moses,

But as for Him, we do not know where He is from.
The blind man replied, This astonishes me!

You do not know where He is from, and yet
He has opened my eyes! We know that God

Does not listen to sinners, but if someone
Fears God and abides by his will, God hears him.

Never before has anyone open the eyes of a man
Born blind. If this Man were not from God,

He could do nothing. To this they replied,
You were born in sin, yet you instruct us?

And they cast him out. When Jesus heard of this,
He found the blind man and asked him,

Do you believe in the Son of Man?
Who is He? the man asked. That I may believe.

Jesus said, You have seen Him, and it is He
With whom you now speak. And he said,

Lord, I believe. And he worshipped Him.
Jesus said, For judgment I came into this world,

That those who do not see may see,
And that those who see may be made blind.

Some Pharisees who stood near to Jesus said,
Are we also blind? Jesus said, If you were blind,

You would be sinless. Yet since you say,
We see, your guilt and your sin remain.

TEN

1.

Verily, verily, I tell you, anyone who does not enter
The sheepfold by the gate but climbs in
Some other way, is a thief.

He that enters by the gate is the shepherd of the sheep.
The gatekeeper opens the gate for him,
And the sheep hear his voice.

He calls his sheep by name and leads them out.
And after he has gathered his flock, he goes before them,
And they follow him, for they know his voice.

They will not follow a stranger. They will flee,
Because they do not know the voice of strangers.
Jesus told them this parable, yet they did not understand

What He told them. Then Jesus said to them,
Verily, verily, I say to you, I am the door of the sheep.
All who come before Me are robbers and thieves,

Yet to them the sheep did not listen.
I am the gate. Those who enter through Me
Will find salvation, and will enter and leave

And find pasture. Thieves seek only to slaughter
And steal, and to destroy. I bring them life in abundance.
I am the good shepherd.

A good shepherd gives his life for his sheep.
A hired man, who is no shepherd, whose sheep
Are not his own, abandons them when he sees

A wolf approach, and the wolf attacks and scatters them.
The man flees because he is a hired hand.
He has no concern for them.

I am the good shepherd.
I know My sheep, and My sheep know me.
As the Father knows Me, so I know the Father;

And I will lay down My life for the sheep.
Other sheep not of this fold are Mine,
I must bring them too. They will hear My voice;

And there will be one flock and one shepherd.
My Father loves Me, because I sacrifice My life
That I may live again. No one takes it from Me;

I give it freely. I have the power to give it
And I have power to take it back.
I received this command from My Father.

2.

Division arose again among the Jews
Because Jesus said these things.
Many said, He has a demon and is mad.

Why do you listen to Him? Others said,
Demons do not speak like this.
Can demons open a blind man's eyes?

3.

Winter came, the time of the Feast of Dedication
In Jerusalem. Jesus walked in the temple,

On Solomon's Porch, and the Jews surrounded him,
And said, How long must You keep us in doubt?

If You are the Christ, tell us.
Jesus answered, I told you, and you do not believe.

The works I do in My Father's name, bear witness of Me.
You do not believe, because you are not My sheep.

My sheep hear My voice, and they follow Me.
I bring them eternal life. They shall never die;

And no one will steal them from My hand.
My Father, who gave them to Me, is greatest,

And no one will take them from My Father's hand,
For I and My Father are one.

Then the Jews again gathered stones
With which to stone Him. Jesus answered them,

I have shown you My Father's many good works.
For which one do you stone Me?

The Jews answered, We do not stone you
For good works, but for blasphemy, and

Because are a Man that pretends to be God.
Jesus answered, Does your law not state,

You are gods? If He called them gods,
To whom God's words came (and the Scripture

Cannot be broken), do you say of Him
The Father sanctifies and sent into the world,

'You blaspheme,' because I said, 'I am the Son of God'?
If My works are not the works of My Father,

Then do not believe Me; but if I do His works,
And you do not believe Me, believe His works,

That you may believe that the Father is in Me, and I in Him.
The Jews again attempted to seize Him,

But He escaped to beyond the Jordan,
To the place where John first baptized.

There He remained. Many came to Him
And said, John performed no signs,

Yet everything he said about Jesus was true.
And many believed in Him there.

ELEVEN

I.

In Bethany, the town of Martha and her sister Mary,
Who anointed the Lord with scented oils and wiped His feet,
Lazarus, their brother, was sick.

Jesus loved Martha and her sister and Lazarus.
The sisters went to Jesus and said, Lord,
The one You love is sick. Jesus said,

This is not a sickness unto death.
It is for the glory of God, that the Son of God
May be glorified by it. Jesus remained

Two more days in Bethany, where Lazarus lay ill.
After this He said to the disciples,
Let us go to Judea again. The disciples said to Him,

Rabbi, the Jews sought to stone You
And You mean to return? Jesus answered,
Are there not twelve hours in the day?

If anyone walks in daylight, he does not stumble,
Because he sees the light of this world.
Yet if one walks at night, he stumbles,

Because there is no light in him.
Our friend Lazarus sleeps. I will go to wake him.
His disciples said, Lord, if he sleeps, he will heal.

Yet the sleep Jesus spoke of was the sleep of death.
Jesus said, Lazarus is dead. And I am glad
That I was not there, that you may believe. Let us go to him.

Thomas the Twin said to his fellow disciples,
Let us go also, that we may join Him in death.
So when Jesus came, He discovered that Lazarus

Had been in the tomb four days.
Bethany was two miles from Jerusalem
And many of the Jews joined the women

Who surrounded Martha and Mary,
To comfort them. Once Martha heard
That Jesus was coming, she went to meet Him

While Mary remained in the house.
Martha said to Jesus, Lord, if You had been here,
My brother would not have died.

But I know that whatever You ask of God,
God will give You. Jesus said to her,
Your brother will rise again.

Martha said, I know that he will rise again
In the resurrection at the last day.
Jesus said, I am the resurrection, and the life:

He that believeth in Me, though he were dead,
Yet shall he live. And whosoever liveth
And believeth in Me shall never die.

Do you believe? She said to Him,
Yes, Lord, I believe that You are the Christ,
The Son of God, who is to come into the world.

And after she said these things, she departed
And in secret went to her sister Mary and said,
The Teacher has come, and He calls for you.

Mary arose quickly and went to Him.
Jesus had not yet entered the town.
He remained in the place where Martha met Him.

The Jews who were with Mary in the house,
Who comforted her, saw Mary rise up quickly.
They believed that she was headed for the tomb

To weep there, and they followed her.
Mary came to Jesus, and when she saw Him,
She fell down at His feet, and said to Him,

Lord, had You been here, my brother would live.
When Jesus saw her weeping, and the Jews
Who came with her weeping,

He groaned in the spirit and was troubled. And He said,
Where have you laid him? They said to Him, Lord,
Come and see. Jesus wept.

Then the Jews said, See how Jesus loved him!
And some said, Why is it that this Man,
Who opened the eyes of the blind,

Could not have kept this man from death?
Then Jesus groaned within, and came to the tomb.
It was a cave, and a heavy stone lay against it.

Jesus said, Remove the stone. Martha said,
Lord, it has been four days, by now there is a stench.
Jesus said, Did I not say tell you that you would see

God's glory if only you believed?
So they took away the stone from the tomb
And Jesus lifted up His eyes and said,

Father, I thank You that You have heard Me.
I know that You always hear Me, yet
Because of these people standing by I said this,

That they may believe that You sent Me.
Jesus cried with a loud voice, Lazarus, come forth!
And Lazarus came out from the tomb,

His hands and feet bound with graveclothes,
And his face wrapped with a cloth.
Jesus said to them, Unbind him, and let him go.

2.

Then many of the Jews who had come to Mary,
And had seen the things Jesus did, believed in Him.
Yet some of them went to the Pharisees

And told them of the things Jesus did.
The chief priests and Pharisees gathered a meeting
Of the Sanhedrin. What shall we do? They said.

This man works many signs.
If we let Him alone like this, everyone will believe in Him,
And the Romans will come and destroy

Our Temple and our nation. Caiaphas,
The high priest, said, You know nothing at all,
Nor do you consider that it is better

That one man should die than that the whole nation
Should perish. Caiaphas did not say this
On his own authority. As high priest

He prophesied that Jesus would die for the nation
And not only for that nation, but also
For the scattered children of God,

Who would be gathered in one place.
From that day forward, the Jews plotted
To put Jesus to death. Because of this,

Jesus no longer walked openly among the Jews.
He journeyed to a city called Ephraim,
In the country near the wilderness,

And there with His disciples He stayed.
Passover neared, and many traveled
Up to Jerusalem before the Passover,

To purify themselves. They sought Jesus,
And spoke among themselves as they stood in the temple,
What do you think—will He not come to the feast?

Both the chief priests and the Pharisees had issued a decree,
That if anyone knew where He was,
He should report it, that they might seize Him.

TWELVE

1.

Six days before Passover,
Jesus arrived in Bethany,
Where Lazarus was raised from the dead.
There they made Him supper;

And Martha served, but Lazarus
Sat at the table with Him.
Then Mary anointed Jesus' feet
With costly oil of spikenard.

She wiped His feet with her hair.
The air was filled with the oil's fragrance.
Then the disciple Judas Iscariot,
Simon's son, who would betray Him, said,

Why was this oil not sold for three hundred
Denarii and given to the poor?
He said this not because he cared for the poor,
But because he was a thief.

He held the money box, and took
Whatever was put in it.
Jesus said, Let her alone; she has kept this oil
For the day of My burial.

The poor will always be with you. I will not.
Many Jews knew that Jesus was in Bethany
And they came to see Him
And to see Lazarus, risen from the dead.

Yet the chief priests plotted
To return Lazarus to the grave
Because his resurrection led many
To believe in Jesus.

2.

The next day a great multitude came to the Passover feast
When they learned that Jesus was coming to Jerusalem.
They gathered branches of palm trees
And went to greet Him, and cried out:

Hosanna! Blessed is He who comes in the name of the Lord!
The King of Israel!
Then Jesus found a young donkey,
And He sat on it; as it is written:

Fear not, daughter of Sion:
Behold, thy King cometh,
Sitting on an ass's colt.
At first, His disciples did not understand,

Yet when Jesus achieved glory,
They remembered that these things
Were written about Him
And that they had done these things to Him.

3.

The people, with Him when He called Lazarus
From his tomb and raised him from the dead,
Bore witness.

For this reason also the people met Him,
Because He had done this sign.

The Pharisees said among themselves,
You see that you accomplish nothing.
Look, the world now follows Him!

4.

Among those who came up to worship at the feast
Were certain Greeks. They approached Philip
From Bethsaida and asked him, We wish to see Jesus.

Philip told Andrew, and together they told Jesus.
Yet Jesus answered, The hour has come
That the Son of Man should be glorified.

I speak in truth, unless a grain of wheat
Falls to the ground and dies, it remains alone;
Yet if it dies, it produces much fruit.

He who loves his life will lose it,
And he who hates his life in this world
Will keep it eternally.

If anyone serves Me, let him follow Me;
Where I am, there also My servant will be.
Those that serve Me, My Father will honor.

Now My soul is troubled. What shall I say?
Father, save Me from this hour? Yet
It was for this purpose that I came to this hour.

Father, glory be Thy name.
Then a voice came from Heaven and said,
I have glorified it and will glorify it once more.

Those near to Him heard the voice
And said that it made the sound of thunder.
Others said, An angel spoke to Him.

Jesus said, This voice did not speak for Me.
It spoke for your sake. Now is the judgment
Of this world; now the ruler of this world

Will be cast out. And if I am lifted up
From this world, I will bring all to Myself.
He said this to signify by the manner of His death.

The people said, The law tells that the Christ
Abides forever; how can You say, The Son of Man
Must be lifted up? Who is this Son of Man?

Jesus said, The light is with you only a little while longer.
Walk while you have the light, lest darkness overtake you.
He who walks in darkness does not know where he is going.

While you have the light, believe in the light,
That you may become children of light.
Jesus spoke, departed, hid from them.

Although He had accomplished many signs
Before them, still they did not believe in Him,
That the word of Isaiah the prophet might be revealed,

Which he spoke: Lord, who has believed our report?
And to whom has the arm of the Lord been revealed?
They could not believe, because again Isaiah said,

He has blinded their eyes and hardened their hearts,
Lest they should see with their eyes,
Lest they should understand with their hearts

And turn, So that I should heal them.
Isaiah said this when he saw His glory
And spoke of Him. Even among the rulers

Many believed in Him, yet because of the Pharisees
They did not confess their faith,
Lest they should be cast out of the synagogue;

For they loved the praise of men
More than the praise of God.
Then Jesus cried out and said,

He who believes in Me, believes not in Me
But in Him who sent Me.
And he who sees Me sees Him who sent Me.

I have come as a light into the world,
That whoever believes in Me
should not abide in darkness.

If anyone hears My words and does not believe,
I do not judge him; for I did not come to condemn
The world but to save the world.

He who rejects Me, and does not receive My teaching,
Has one who judges him—the word I spoke
Will condemn him in the last day.

I do not speak on My own authority;
The Father who sent Me gave Me commandment—
What I should say and what I should speak.

I know that His command is everlasting life.
Therefore, whatever I speak,
Just as the Father has told Me, so I speak.

TRANSEPT

THIRTEEN

Before the Passover feast, Jesus knew
That His hour had come, and He should leave
This world to His Father. He loved His own
In this world. He loved them to the end.
And supper ended, the devil already put it into

The heart of Judas Iscariot, Simon's son,
To betray Him. And Jesus, knowing that the Father
Gave all things into His hands, and that
He came from God and would return to God,
Got up from supper and removed His garments,

Took a towel and tied it around His waist.
He poured water into a basin, and began to wash
The disciples' feet, and dry them with the towel He wore.
He came to Simon Peter. And Peter said, Lord,
Do You wash my feet? Jesus answered,

What I do you do not presently understand,
Yet you will know hereafter. Peter said to Him,
No. You will never wash my feet!
Jesus said, If I do not, you have no part with Me.
Simon Peter said to Him, Lord, not my feet only,

But also my hands and my head!
Jesus said to him, He who is bathed
Needs only to wash his feet, but is completely clean;
And you are clean, but not all of you.
After He washed their feet, He took His garments,

Resumed his place, and said to them,
Do you know what I have done to you?
You call me Teacher and Lord, and
You are correct, as I am. If I then,
As your Lord and Teacher, wash your feet,

So you ought to wash one another's.
For I have provided you with an example,
That you should do as I have done to you.
Truly, I tell you, a slave is no greater
Than his master; nor is He who is sent

Greater than He who sent Him.
If you know these things, you are blessed
If you do them. I do not speak concerning all of you.
I know whom I have chosen; yet that
The Scripture may be fulfilled, *He who eats bread with Me*

Has lifted up his heel against Me.
I tell you this now, before it comes to pass,
That when it occurs, you may believe that I am He.
Truly, I say to you, he who receives whomever I send receives Me;
And he who receives Me receives Him who sent Me.

When Jesus said these things,
He became troubled in spirit, and testified,
Truly, I say to you, one of you will betray Me.
The disciples looked at one another, confused
About which disciple He spoke.

Leaning on Jesus' chest was the disciple
Whom Jesus loved. Simon Peter asked Jesus
Of whom He spoke. Then, as the disciple leaned back
From Jesus' breast, he said, Lord, who is it?
Jesus said, It is he to whom I shall give

A piece of bread dipped it. And having dipped
The bread, He gave it to Judas Iscariot,
The son of Simon. Satan entered him.
Then Jesus said, What you do, do quickly.
Yet none knew for what reason He said this.

Some thought, because Judas had the money box,
That Jesus had said, Purchase what we need
For the feast, or to give something to the poor.
Judas, having received the piece of bread,
Went out immediately. And it was night.

Jesus said, Now the Son of Man is glorified,
And God is glorified in Him. If God is glorified
In Him, God will also glorify Him in Himself,
And glorify Him immediately. Little children,
I will be with you only a little while longer.

You will seek Me; and as I said to the Jews,
Where I go, you cannot come. So now I say to you.
I have given you a new commandment:
That you love one another; as I have loved you,
That you also love one another. By this

All will know that you are My disciples,
If you have love for one another.
Simon Peter said to Him, Lord, where are You going?
Jesus said, Where I go you cannot follow Me now,
But you shall follow Me afterward.

Peter said, Lord, why can I not follow You now?
I will lay down my life for Your sake.
Jesus said, Will you lay down your life for My sake?
Truly, I say to you, the rooster shall not crow
Till you have denied Me three times.

FOURTEEN

Do not let your heart be troubled.
If you believe in God, you also believe in Me.
In My Father's house there are many rooms.
If this was untrue, I would have told you.
I go to prepare a place for you.
And if I go and prepare a place for you,

I will return and receive you unto Myself.
That where I am, there you may be also.
And you will know the place I go to.
Thomas said, Lord, we do not know
To where You go. How can we know the way?
Jesus said, I am the way, the truth, and the life.

No one comes to the Father except through Me.
If you knew Me, you would also know My Father.
Now you know Him and see Him.
Philip said, Lord, show us the Father,
And it will suffice. Jesus said,
I have been with you so long, and yet

You do not know Me, Philip? He who has seen Me
Has also seen the Father; so how can you say,
Show us the Father? Do you not believe
That I am in the Father, and the Father in Me?
The words that I speak to you I do not speak
On My own authority; but the Father who dwells in Me

Does the works. Believe Me that I am
In the Father and the Father in Me, or else
Believe Me for the sake of the works themselves.
Truly, I say to you, he who believes in Me,
The works that I do he will do also;
And greater works than these he will do,

Because I go to My Father. And whatever you ask
In My name, I will do, that the Father may be Glorified in the Son.
If you ask anything in My name,
I will do it. If you love Me, you will keep
My commandments. And I will ask the Father,
And He will give you another Paraclete,

That He may abide with you forever—
The Spirit of Truth, whom the world cannot receive,
Because it does not see Him or know Him;
Yet you know Him. He dwells with and in you.
I will not leave you as orphans;
I will come back to you. A little while longer

And the world will no longer see Me,
Yet you will see Me. Because I live, you will live also.
On that day you will know that I am in My Father,
And you in Me, and I in you.
He who has My commandments and keeps them,
It is he who loves Me. And he who loves Me

Will be loved by My Father, and I will love him
And reveal Myself to him. Judas (not Iscariot)
Said, Lord, How is it that You will manifest Yourself to us,
And not to the world? Jesus said,
If anyone loves Me, he will keep My word;
My Father will love him, and We will come to him

And make Our dwelling with him.
He who does not love Me does not keep My words;
And the word which you hear is not Mine
But that of Father who sent Me. These things
I speak to you while in your presence.
Yet the Paraclete, the Holy Spirit,

Whom the Father will send in My name,
He will teach you all things, and bring to your
Remembrance all things that I said to you.
Peace I leave with you, My peace I give to you;
I do not give to you as the world gives.
Let not your heart be troubled, neither let it be afraid.

You heard Me tell you, I am going away
And will return to you. If you loved Me,
You would rejoice because I said,
I am going to the Father, for My Father
Is greater than I. And now I have told you
Before it comes, that when it does come to pass,

You may believe. I will not speak with you
Much longer, for the ruler of this world
Approaches, and he has no power over Me.
Yet that the world may know that I love the Father,
And I do as the Father commands.
Arise, let us leave this place.

FIFTEEN

I am the true vine, and My Father is the vinedresser.
Every branch of Mine that remains fruitless is pruned,
That it may bring more fruit forth. You are clean already
By the words that I have spoken to you.

Abide in Me, and I will abide in you.
As the branch cannot bear fruit of itself,
Unless it abides in the vine, neither can you,
Unless you abide in Me. I am the vine; you are the branches.

He who abides in Me, and I in him, bears much fruit;
For without Me you can do nothing. If a man does not
Abide in Me, he is cast forth as a branch and withers;
And they are gathered, thrown into the fire, and burned.

If you abide in Me, and My words abide in you,
You will ask for what you desire, and it shall be done for you.
In this way My Father is glorified, that you bear much fruit;
So you prove to be My disciples.

As the Father loved Me, I have loved you; abide in My love.
Keep My commandments, and you will abide in My love,
Just as I have kept My Father's commandments
And abide in His. These things I have spoken to you,

That My joy may be in you, and that your joy may be complete.
This is My commandment, that you love one another
As I have loved you. Man has no greater love than this,
That a man lay down his life for his friends.

If you do as I command, then you are My friends.
I will no longer call you servants, for a servant
Does not know what his master does;
Yet I have called you friends, for all that I have heard

From My Father I have made known to you.
You did not choose Me, but I chose you and appointed you
That you should go and bear fruit, and that your fruit abide,
That what you ask the Father in My name He may give to you.

These things I command you, that you love one another.
If the world hates you, you know that it hated Me
Before it hated you. If you were of the world,
The world would love its own.

Yet because you are not of the world, I chose you
Out of the world, therefore the world hates you.
Remember the words that I said to you,
A slave is not greater than his master.

If they persecuted Me, they will also persecute you.
If they kept My word, they will keep yours also.
Yet all these things they will do to you for My name's sake,
Because they do not know Him who sent Me.

If I had not come and spoken to them, they would have no sin,
But now they have no excuse for their sin.
He who hates Me hates My Father also.
If I had not done among them works which no one else did,

They would have no sin; but now they have seen
And also hated both Me and My Father.
Yet this happened that the word might be fulfilled
That is written in their law: They hated Me without a cause.

Yet when the Paraclete comes, whom I shall send to you,
The Spirit of truth who proceeds from the Father,
He will testify of Me. And you also will bear witness,
Because you have been with Me from the beginning.

SIXTEEN

I speak these things to you, so that you do not fail.
They will drive you from the synagogues.
Indeed, the time will come when whoever kills you
Believes that he does the will of the Lord.

They will do these things to you because they do not know
The Father nor Me. Yet I have instructed you so that
When the time arrives, you will remember that I told you.
And I waited until now to tell you, for I was with you

In the beginning. Now I must go to Him who sent Me,
And still none of you inquires, To where do I go?
Your hearts are filled with sorrow because of what I tell you.
Yet it is the truth. It is far better for you that I depart,

For if I do not, the Paraclete will not come to your aid.
But if I depart, I will send Him to you. And when He arrives,
He will convict the world of sin, and righteousness,
And judgment. Of sin, because they do not believe in Me;

Of righteousness, as I go to My Father and am seen no more;
Of judgment, because the ruler of this world is judged.
There remains much for Me to tell you, yet you cannot bear
To listen now. Know this: when the Paraclete arrives,

He will lead you into truth. He will speak not on His own
Authority, but whatever He hears He will speak of;
And He will tell you of what is still to come. He will glorify Me,
For He will take what is Mine and declare it to you.

All things that the Father has are Mine.
You will not see Me for a little while, and in a little while
You will see Me again, because I go to the Father.
Then some disciples said among themselves,

What is this that He says to us, A little while,
And you will not see Me; a little while later
You will see Me; and, Because I go to the Father?
We do not understand. Jesus knew that they wanted

To ask Him, and He said to them, Do you speak
Among yourselves about what I said, A little while,
And you will not see Me; and again a little while later,
And you will see Me? Truly, I say to you that though

You will weep and lament, the world will rejoice,
And though you sorrow, that sorrow will turn to joy.
When a woman is in labor, she sorrows for her hour
Of birth has come, yet as soon as she gives birth,

In her joy for a new human life, she forgets her anguish.
Though you now have sorrow, you will rejoice
At My return, and none can take this joy from you.
On that day, you will ask Me nothing. Truly, I say to you,

Whatever is asked of the Father in My name will be given.
Until this moment, you have asked for nothing in My name.
Ask, and ye shall receive, that your joy may be complete.
I have said these things to you in a strange language,

Yet the time will come when I will speak plainly of the Father.
On that day, you will ask in My name, and I will not say
That I pray to the Father on your behalf, for the Father
Loves you, because you have loved Me, and believed

That I came forth from Him. I came forth from the Father
And come into the world. I leave the world and go to the Father.
Jesus's disciples said to Him, You speak plainly now
And use no strange language. Now we are certain

That You know all, and do not have any need for questions.
In this we believe that You have come from God.
Jesus said, Now do you believe? The hour will soon arrive,
Indeed, it has already, that you will each be scattered,

And leave Me. Yet I am not alone, for the Father is with Me.
I have said this to you, that in Me you may find peace.
In this world you will find only trials and tribulations,
Yet be strong and undaunted. I have overcome the world.

SEVENTEEN

Jesus spoke these words,
Raised His eyes to Heaven,
And said: Father, the hour has come.

Glorify Your Son, that Your Son
Also may glorify You,
As You have given Him

Authority over all flesh,
That He should give eternal life
To as many as You have given Him.

And this is eternal life,
That they may know You,
The only true God, and Jesus Christ

Whom You have sent.
I have glorified You on the earth.
I have finished the work

That You have given Me to do.
And now, O Father, glorify Me
Together with Yourself,

With the glory which I had
With You before the world was.
I have made manifest Your name

To the men in this world
That You have given Me.
They have kept Your word.

You have given Me all things.
For the words I speak
Are the words You gave to me

And they received them,
And know that I came forth
From you; and they believed

That You sent me to them.
I do not pray for the world,
But I do pray for them

Whom You gave to me,
For they are Yours to give.
All that is Mine is Yours,

And all that is Yours is Mine,
And glorifies Me.
Now I am no longer in this world,

Yet these are, and I come to You.
Holy Father, keep through Your name
Those whom You have given Me,

That they, as We, are one.
While I was with them in the world,
I kept them in Your name.

Those whom You gave Me
I have kept; and none of them is lost except
The Son of perdition,

That Scripture might be fulfilled.
Now I come to You,
And these things I speak in the world,

That they may have My joy
Fulfilled in themselves.
I gave them Your word;

And the world has hated them
Because they are not of the world,
Just as I am not of the world.

I do not pray that You should take them
Out of the world,
But that You should keep them

From the evil one.
They are not of the world,
Just as I am not of the world.

Sanctify them by Your truth.
For Your word is Truth.
As You sent Me into the world,

I also sent them into the world.
And for their sakes
I sanctify Myself, that they also

May be sanctified by the truth.
I do not pray for these alone,
But also for those who will believe in Me

Through their word;
That they all may be one,
As You, Father, are in Me, and I in You;

That they also may be one in Us,
That the world may believe
That You sent Me.

And the glory which You gave Me
I have given them,
That they may be one just as We are one:

I in them, and You in Me;
That they may be made perfect in one,
And that the world may know

That You have sent Me,
And have loved them
As You have loved Me.

O Father, I desire that they also
Whom You gave to Me
May be with Me where I am,

That they may behold My glory
Which You have given Me;
For You loved Me

Before the foundation of the world.
O Father of righteousness!
The world has not known You,

Yet I have known You;
And they know that You sent Me.
And I have declared to them Your name,

And will declare it that the love
With which You loved Me
May be in them, and I in them.

ALTAR

EIGHTEEN

Jesus spoke these words, then went with His disciples
To the Brook Kidron, where there was an olive grove.

Which they entered. And Judas, the betrayer, knew this place,
For Jesus often met there with His disciples.

Then Judas, with a contingent of Roman soldiers,
And officials from the chief priests and Pharisees,

Arrived there with lanterns, torches, and weapons.
Jesus, who knew all things that would come upon Him,

Went forward among them and said to them,
Whom do you seek? They answered, Jesus of Nazareth.

Jesus said, I am He. And Judas, who betrayed Him,
Stood with them. When Jesus said, I am He,

They drew back and fell to the ground.
He asked again, Whom do you seek? And they said, again,

Jesus of Nazareth. Jesus said, I told you that I am He.
Therefore, if you seek Me, let these men go their way,

That the saying might be fulfilled which He spoke,
Of those whom You gave Me I have lost none.

Then Simon Peter drew his sword and struck Malchus,
The servant of the High Priest, and cut off his right ear.

Jesus said to Peter, Return your sword into its sheath.
Shall I not drink the cup which My Father has given Me?

Then the troops and the captain and the officers of the Jews
Arrested Jesus and bound Him. And they led Him away

To Annas first, for he was the father-in-law of Caiaphas,
The high priest that year. Caiaphas advised the Jews

That it was expedient that one man should die for the people.
Simon Peter followed Jesus, and so did another disciple.

That disciple was known to Annas,
And went with Jesus into the courtyard of the high priest.

Peter stood at the door outside. Then the other disciple,
Who was known to Annas, went out and spoke

To her who kept the door, and brought Peter in.
Then the servant girl who kept the door said to Peter,

You are not also one of this Man's disciples, are you?
He said, I am not. It was cold, and the servants and officers

Made a fire of coals, and they warmed themselves.
And Peter stood with them and warmed himself.

Annas then asked Jesus about His disciples
And His doctrine. Jesus answered, I spoke openly

To the world. I always taught in synagogues
And in the temple, where the Jews always meet,

And in secret I have said nothing. Why do you ask Me?
Ask those who have heard Me what I said to them.

They know what I said. And when He had said these things,
One of the officers who stood by struck Jesus

With the palm of his hand, saying, Is that how you answer
Annas? Jesus answered him, If I have spoken evil,

Bear witness of the evil; but if I speak properly,
Why do you strike Me? Then Annas sent Him bound

To Caiaphas the high priest. Now Simon Peter stood
And warmed himself. Therefore they said to him,

You are not also one of His disciples, are you?
He denied it and said, No, I am not. One of the servants

Of the high priest, a relative of Malchus, said,
Did I not see you in the garden with Him?

Peter denied again. A rooster crowed.
Then they led Jesus from Caiaphas to the Praetorium.

It was early morning. Yet they did not go into the Praetorium,
For fear of defilement, that they might eat the Passover.

Pilate then went out to them and said,
What accusation do you bring against this Man?

They answered, If He were not a criminal,
We would not have delivered Him up to you.

Then Pilate said, Take Him and judge Him
According to your law. The Jews said to him,

It is not lawful for us to put anyone to death.
This would fulfill the word of Jesus, which He spoke,

Signifying by what death He would die.
Pilate again entered the Praetorium, called forth Jesus,

And said to Him, Are You the King of the Jews?
Jesus answered, Do you speak for yourself,

Or did others tell you this concerning Me?
Pilate responded, Am I a Jew? Your own nation

And its chief priests have delivered You to me.
What have You done? Jesus said, My kingdom is not of this world.

If My kingdom were of this world, My servants would fight,
So that I should not be delivered to the Jews;

Yet now My kingdom is not from here. Pilate said,
Are You a king? Jesus said, You say rightly that I am a king.

For this cause I was born, and for this cause
I have come into the world, that I should bear witness

To the truth, everyone who belongs to the truth
Hears My voice. Pilate said, What is truth?

And when he had said this, he went out again to the Jews,
And said to them, I find no fault in Him at all,

Yet you Jews have a custom that I should release
Someone to you at the Passover.

Do you therefore want me to release to you
the King of the Jews?

They all cried again, saying,
Not this Man, but Barabbas, the robber!

NINETEEN

I.

Pilate took Jesus and scourged Him.
And the soldiers twisted together a crown of thorns

And placed it on His head and dressed Him a purple robe.
Then they said, Hail, King of the Jews! And struck Him with their hands.

Pilate then went out again, and said to the Jews,
Behold, I bring Him out to you, that you may know

That I find no fault in Him. Then Jesus came out,
Wearing the crown of thorns and the purple robe.

And Pilate said, Behold the Man!
When the chief priests and officers saw Him,

They cried out, Crucify Him, crucify Him!
Pilate said, Take Him and crucify Him. I find no fault in Him.

The Jews said, By our law He ought to die,
Because He made Himself the Son of God.

When Pilate heard that saying, he was the more afraid.
He went into the Praetorium, and said to Jesus,

Where are You from? Jesus gave him no answer.
Then Pilate said to Him, Will You not respond to me?

Do You not know that I have power to crucify You,
And the power to release You? Jesus answered,

You could have no power at all against Me unless
It was given you from above. The one who delivered Me

To you has the greater sin. From then on,
Pilate sought to release Him, but the Jews cried out,

If you let this Man go, you are not Caesar's friend!
Anyone who declares himself a king opposes Caesar!

When Pilate heard this, he brought Jesus out
And sat down in the judgment seat in a place called

The Pavement, but in Hebrew, Gabbatha.
Now it was the Preparation Day of the Passover,

And about the sixth hour. And he said to the Jews,
Behold your King! But they cried out, Away with Him,

Away with Him! Crucify Him! Pilate said to them,
Shall I crucify your King? The chief priests answered,

We have no king but Caesar! Then Pilate delivered Him
To the Jews to be crucified. So they took Jesus and led Him away.

And He, carrying His Cross, went out to a place
Called the Place of a Skull, called in Hebrew, Golgotha,

Where they crucified Him, and two others with Him,
One on either side, and Jesus in the midst.

Pilate wrote a title and put it on the Cross:
JESUS OF NAZARETH, THE KING OF THE JEWS.

Then many of the Jews read this title,
As the place where Jesus was crucified was near the city,

And the sign was written in Hebrew, Greek, and Latin.
The chief priests of the Jews said to Pilate,

Do not write, The King of the Jews, but,
He said, I am the King of the Jews.

Pilate replied, What I have written, I have written.
Then the soldiers, when they had crucified Jesus,

Took His garments and made four parts,
To each soldier a part, and also the seamless tunic.

They said, Let us not tear the tunic, but cast lots for it,
Whose it shall be, that the Scripture might be fulfilled:

They divided My garments among them,
And for My clothing cast lots.

2.

Now there stood near to the Cross of Jesus His mother,
And His mother's sister, Mary the wife of Clopas,

And Mary Magdalene. And when Jesus saw His mother,
And the disciple whom He loved standing by her,

He said to His mother, Woman, behold your son!
Then He said to the disciple, Behold your mother!

And from that hour that disciple took her to his own home.
Jesus, who knew then that all things were accomplished,

And that the Scripture might be fulfilled, said, I thirst!
A vessel full of posca stood there;

And they filled a sponge with posca,
Placed it on a branch of hyssop, and lifted it to His mouth.

When Jesus received the posca, He said, It is finished!
And bowed His head, and gave up the ghost.

3.

Because it was the Preparation Day, and the bodies
Should not remain on the Cross on the Sabbath

(For that Sabbath was a high day), the Jews asked Pilate
That their legs might be broken, and that they might be taken away.

Then soldiers came and broke the legs of the first
And of the other who was crucified with Him.

But when they came to Jesus and saw that He was dead,
They did not break His legs. Instead, one of the soldiers

Pierced His side with a spear, and out came blood and water.
And he who witnesses this has testified to its truth,

So that you may believe. These things happened
So that the Scripture should be fulfilled:

Not one of His bones shall be broken.
They shall look on Him whom they pierced.

After this, Joseph of Arimathea, being a disciple of Jesus,
Secretly, for fear of the Jews, asked Pilate

That he might take away the body of Jesus;
And Pilate gave him permission.

So he came and took the body of Jesus.
Nicodemus, who at first came to Jesus by night, also came,

And brought with him a mixture of myrrh and aloes,
About a hundred pounds. Then they took the body of Jesus,

And bound it in strips of linen with the spices,
As is the custom of the Jews to bury.

Now the place where He was crucified there was a garden,
And in the garden a new tomb in which no one had yet been laid.

So there they laid Jesus, because of the Jews' Preparation Day,
For the tomb was close at hand.

APSE

TWENTY

1.

Early on the first day of the week,
Mary Magdalene went to the tomb
While it was still dark, and saw

The stone removed from it.
She ran to Simon Peter and to the disciple
Whom Jesus loved, and said to them,

They have taken away the Lord
Out of the tomb, and we do not know
Where they have laid Him.

Peter and the other disciple went to the tomb.
They ran, and the other disciple ran faster,
And was first to arrive at the tomb.

He bent down to look inside and beheld
The linens lying there, yet did not go in.
Then Simon Peter arrived and went inside.

He did see the linens, and also the soudarion
That was upon His head, alone and neatly folded.
The other disciple who came first to the tomb

Entered, and he saw, and believed.
For they did not yet understand the scripture,
That Jesus must arise from the dead.

The disciples left and returned to their homes.
Mary remained outside the tomb and wept,
And as she wept, she bent down to look inside the tomb.

And she beheld two angels in white,
One seated at the head and the other at the feet
Where the body of Jesus once laid. They asked her,

Woman, why do you weep? She said to them,
They have taken away my Lord,
And I do not know where they laid Him.

After she spoke, she turned to leave,
And saw Jesus next to her, yet she did not
Recognize Him. Jesus asked her, Woman,

Why do you weep? Who is it that you seek?
She thought that He might be the gardener,
And said, Sir, if you have removed Him,

Tell me where He is laid, and I will gather Him.
Mary, Jesus said. She turned to face Him
And cried, Rabboni! Jesus said, Do not cling to me,

For I am not yet ascended
To My Father, and to your Father,
And to My God, and to your God.

Mary went to the disciples and told them,
I have seen the Lord, and told them
What He said to her. That evening,

The disciples gathered together,
And shut the doors from fear of the Judeans.
Jesus came and stood among them

And said, Peace be with you.
He showed them the wounds in His hands
And His side. The disciples rejoiced

When they saw the Lord. Again He said,
Peace be with you. As the Father sent me,
So I will send you. He breathed on them

And said, Receive the Holy Spirit.
Whose sins you forgive are forgiven
And if forgiveness is withheld, it is withheld.

One of the Twelve, Thomas, called Didymus
(The Twin), was not with them when Jesus came.
The disciples told him, We have seen the Lord.

Yet Thomas said, Except that I shall see
In His hands the mark of nails,
And put my finger into the wound, and thrust my hand

Into His side, I will not believe.
Eight days later, His disciples were inside,
And Thomas was with them.

Although the doors were locked,
Jesus came and stood among them and said,
Peace be with you. Then He said to Thomas,

Place your finger here, and see My hands;
And take your hand and put it into My side;
And do not continue in disbelief, but believe.

Thomas said, My Lord and God.
Jesus said, Thomas, because you have seen Me, you believe.
Blessed are those who have not seen and yet believe.

2.

Jesus performed many other signs in the presence of the disciples not recorded in this book. These are written that you may believe that Jesus is the Christ, the Son of God, and that in this belief you may have eternal life in His name.

TWENTY-ONE

1.

After this, Jesus appeared again to the disciples
At the Sea of Tiberias. Simon Peter, Thomas the Twin,
Nathanael of Cana in Galilee, Zebedee's sons,
And two others were together.

Simon Peter said, I go to fish. They said to him,
We will go with you. They got into the boat.
Yet they caught nothing. When morning came,
Jesus stood on the shore.

The disciples saw Him yet did not know that it was Jesus.
Jesus said, Children, do you have you any food?
No, they said. And He said, Cast your net
On the boat's right side, and you will find some.

So they cast the net, and could not draw it in
Due to the multitude of fish. The disciple
Whom Jesus loved said to Simon Peter, It is the Lord!
Simon Peter put back on his coat and leapt into the sea.

Yet the other disciples came in the little boat
(They were two hundred cubits from shore),
And dragged the net heavy with fish.
Once at shore, they saw a coal fire,

With fish cooking upon it, and loaves of fresh bread.
Jesus said, Bring Me some of the fish you caught.
Simon Peter dragged the heavy net to land,
Full of large fish, one hundred and fifty-three.

Despite this weight, the net remained unbroken.
Jesus said, Come eat with Me. The disciples
Dared not ask him who He was, for they knew
It was the Lord. Jesus gave them bread and fish.

This was the third time Jesus showed Himself
To His disciples after He rose from the dead.
After they had eaten, Jesus said to Simon Peter,
Simon, son of Jonah, do you love Me more than these?

Simon Peter answered Him, Yes, Lord;
You know that I love You. Jesus said to him,
Feed My lambs. Then he said again, Simon,
Son of Jonah, do you love Me? Simon Peter said to Him,

Yes, Lord; You know that I love You.
Jesus said to him, Tend My sheep.
Jesus said to him a third time, Simon,
Son of Jonah, do you love Me?

Simon Peter grieved that Jesus asked him yet again.
And he said, Lord, You know all things;
You know that I love You. Jesus said to him,
Feed My sheep. Truly, I say to you,

When you were younger, you wore your belt
And walked wherever you wished;
Yet when you are old, you will stretch out your hands,
And another will tie your belt and carry you

Where you do not wish to go. Jesus said this
To illustrate the kind of death that would glorify God.
Then He said to Simon Peter, Follow Me.
Then Simon Peter turned and saw the disciple

Whom Jesus loved, who had leaned against
Jesus' breast at the supper, and He said,
Lord, who will betray You? Simon Peter, seeing him,
Said to Jesus, But Lord, what shall this man do?

Jesus said, If I will that he remain till I come,
What is that to you? You follow Me.
Rumor spread that this disciple would not die.
Yet Jesus did not say that he would not die,

He said, If I will that he remain till I come,
What is that to you? This is the disciple
Who testifies of these things, and wrote them down;
And we know that his testimony is true.

2.

And there are also many other things that Jesus did, which if all were written one by one, I suppose that even the world itself could not contain the books that would be written. Amen.

ABOUT THE AUTHOR

ERIC HOFFMAN is the author of several books of poetry, including, most recently, *Inscribed Red: Haiku Versions After Akutagawa Ryūnosuke* (Spuyten Duyvil, 2024), a translation of Sumitaku Kenshin's *Unfinished* (Spuyten Duyvil, 2023), and *Circumference of the Sun* (Dos Madres Press, 2021). He edited a new edition of Philip Pain's *Daily Meditations* (Spuyten Duyvil, 2021) and is the author of *Oppen: A Narrative* (Shearsman, 2011, rev. ed. Spuyten Duyvil, 2018), a biography of poet George Oppen, among numerous other works. He lives in Connecticut.

Other books by Eric Hoffman
published by Dos Madres Press

Life at Braintree (2008)
The American Eye (2011)
By the Hours (2013)
Forms of Life (2015)
Presence of Life (2018)
Circumference of the Sun (2021)

He is also included in:
Realms of the Mothers:
The First Decade of Dos Madres Press (2016)

For the full Dos Madres Press catalog:
www.dosmadres.com

www.ingramcontent.com/pod-product-compliance
Lightning Source LLC
Chambersburg PA
CBHW051630120626
46551CB00014B/2017